Robert Fulton:

Engineer of the Steamboat

by Don Herweck

Science Contributor
Sally Ride Science
Science Consultants
Michael E. Koecky, Science Educator
Jane Weir, Physicist

First hardcover edition published in 2009 by
Compass Point Books
151 Good Counsel Drive
P.O. Box 669
Mankato, MN 56002-0669

Editor: Mari Bolte
Designer: Heidi Thompson
Editorial Contributor: Sue Vander Hook

Art Director: LuAnn Ascheman-Adams
Creative Director: Keith Griffin
Editorial Director: Nick Healy
Managing Editor: Catherine Neitge

 This book was manufactured with paper containing at least 10 percent post-consumer waste.

Library of Congress Cataloging-in-Publication Data
Herweck, Don.
 Robert Fulton : engineer of the steamboat / by Don Herweck.
   p. cm. — (Mission: Science)
 Includes index.
 ISBN 978-0-7565-3961-0 (library binding)
 1. Fulton, Robert, 1765–1815—Juvenile literature.
 2. Marine engineers—United States—Biography—Juvenile literature. 3. Inventors—United States—
Biography—Juvenile literature. 4. Steamboats—United States—History—19th century—Juvenile
literature. I. Title. II. Series.
 VM140.F9H47 2008
 623.82'4092—dc22
 [B]   2008007728

Visit Compass Point Books on the Internet at *www.compasspointbooks.com*
or e-mail your request to *custserv@compasspointbooks.com*

Table of Contents

Maiden Voyage

People on the dock thought Robert Fulton's boat was a ridiculous idea. They had never seen a vessel powered by an engine, and they were quick to dub it "Fulton's Folly." Others were amazed at this long, thin boat with a huge paddle wheel on each side.

It was August 17, 1807, a warm summer day, when 40 well-dressed New Yorkers boarded this unusual boat. Black smoke belched from the stack as the vessel left New York City and headed up the Hudson River. Nearly 24 hours later, the boat docked near Germantown at the Clermont estate. The passengers, who were guests of Robert Livingston, the owner of the estate and Fulton's business partner, stayed there that night.

But the journey wasn't over. The next morning, the boat headed north to Albany, where a small enthusiastic crowd hailed the historic maiden voyage. Fulton's steamboat, later called the *Clermont* by the press, was a success. It had traveled a record 150 miles (240 kilometers) in 32 hours and averaged 4.7 miles (7.5 km) per hour.

Fulton and Livingston quickly set up commercial steamboat travel on the Hudson River. Fulton's invention changed how people traveled, expanded commerce, and helped America grow.

Robert Fulton and Robert Livingston had a steamboat built in 1803 that ended up sinking. Their efforts were finally successful with the construction of the *Clermont*.

Fulton and Newton

A good engineer like Robert Fulton designed his steamboat according to Sir Isaac Newton's (1643–1727) laws of motion. Newton's laws, as they are called, explain the effects of force on motion. Fulton used a steam engine (the force) to turn a paddle wheel, which in turn moved the boat, and Newton's third law did the rest. The law states that for every action, there is an equal and opposite reaction. In other words, the steamboat moved at a rate equal to the energy produced by the steam engine.

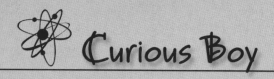

Curious Boy

The steamboat wasn't Fulton's first interest. He had been a curious inventor since he was a young boy. Robert Fulton was born on November 14, 1765, on a farm in Little Britain (now called Fulton), Pennsylvania. When he was 8, his family moved 20 miles (32 km) north to Lancaster, where his father worked as a tailor. Two years later, Robert's father died, leaving his wife and five children in poverty. Robert tried living with an uncle for a while, but soon returned home to his mother.

The school Robert attended was very strict. Robert wasn't very interested in the lessons. His mother was concerned that her son wasn't learning enough, but the teacher said there wasn't much he could do. He said Robert's "head was so full of original ideas that there was no room for ... the contents of dusty books."

Robert enjoyed figuring things out for himself. He made

The Revolutionary War had begun in 1775 when Robert was 10 years old.

lead pencils out of graphite and household utensils for his mother, and experimented with the liquid metal mercury.

By watching the local gunsmiths, Robert learned how to make guns. But he also suggested how they could improve their guns. He drew detailed designs for new models. One of his ideas was for an air gun that fired ammunition by using compressed air. His inventor's mind was already at work.

Early Steam Engine

The steam engine was not a new invention in Fulton's time. The idea of using the power of steam dates back to the first century, when engineer and inventor Hero of Alexandria designed an engine powered by steam. His invention worked something like a modern-day jet engine. Fulton was later credited with successfully putting a steam engine into practical commercial use.

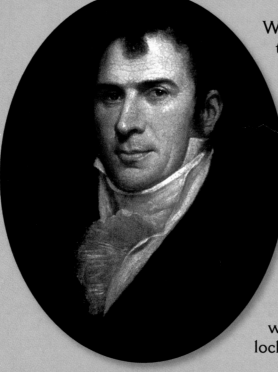

When Robert was 14, he moved to Philadelphia, about 65 miles (104 km) east of Lancaster. There he worked as an apprentice to a jeweler. He also learned to weave hair into fancy designs with beautiful pieces of jewelry. But his favorite work was painting miniature portraits.

Since there were no cameras, people hired artists to paint tiny portraits that would fit into small cases or lockets. Robert eventually started his own portrait business and set his sights on a career in art.

Fulton's Birthplace

The house where Fulton was born in 1765 burned down in 1822. Later it was rebuilt to look like the original. Tours, special events, and fairs are conducted at this historical site where a bit of Fulton's childhood is displayed.

Did You Know?

Only a few pieces of Fulton's artwork still exist. Some of his miniature portraits are owned by the Pennsylvania Historical Society in Philadelphia.

▲ King George III founded the Royal Academy of Arts in 1768.

At the age of 21, Fulton was still serious about becoming a famous artist. In 1786, he went to London, where he studied under artist Benjamin West. Fulton's paintings showed promise, and two of them were displayed at the Royal Academy of Arts in London.

But making a living as an artist was difficult. Fulton often had trouble paying his rent. He had met some influential people in London, however. Their mutual interests in mechanics and inventions would change the course of Fulton's life.

The Earl of Stanhope had a huge influence on Robert Fulton's life. Fulton became interested in what this upper-class inventor was designing, including a carriage and a boat powered by steam. Stanhope never built his designs. But he told Fulton about them and about a steam engine recently built by engineers Matthew Boulton and James Watt.

Another prominent friend, the Duke of Bridgewater, introduced Fulton to man-made waterways called canals. Fulton began looking for better ways to transport goods and people by using canals. He calculated boat speeds and water and wind resistance to better understand the mechanics of water travel.

Many years after Fulton's lifetime, the Panama Canal locks were constructed to raise or lower vessels by controlling the water level.

Canal to the World

More than 60 years after Fulton's death, work began on one of the largest and most complex engineering feats ever attempted.

Canals are artificial waterways used for shipping and travel. The Panama Canal stretches 50 miles (80 km) and links the Atlantic and Pacific oceans in Central America. By traversing the canal, rather than going around South America, ships can shave more than 7,740 miles (12,480 km) off their voyage.

The project first began in 1880 under French supervision. It was completed in 1914 by the United States. In 1999, the United States gave Panama control of the canal.

This very successful canal is used to shorten sea routes for commercial and cruise ships. It eliminates the dangerous route around Cape Horn on the southern tip of South America.

More than 80,000 workers were involved with the building of the Panama Canal. Around 30,000 workers died between 1880 and 1914.

In 1796, Fulton wrote a book titled *Treatise on the Improvement of Canal Navigation*. It included calculations and drawings of boats and inclined planes. U.S. President George Washington received a copy of the book and wrote to Fulton. Fulton believed a small canal system would improve transportation in the United States.

British leaders liked Fulton's ideas and hired him to improve England's canals. They were glad to have better ways to move coal from the mines to the cities.

Fulton worked on canals for many years. He used the double inclined plane to raise and lower boats in canals. Shaped like a wedge, an inclined plane allows heavy loads to be raised with less energy and effort.

Fulton developed a system where a plane was used to raise a boat. Another plane lowered boats at the same time. Fulton's design used water energy and pulleys with chains to lift and lower boats. He also designed a way to hoist boats up hills between canals.

Fulton's double inclined plane made it much easier to lower and lift boats into and out of the water.

Canal Clean Up

Today there are numerous canal systems throughout the United States. When weather damages canals, cleanup and rebuilding must take place in order for ships to continue using them.

In 2005, Hurricane Katrina struck the United States. It was one of the five most destructive hurricanes in the history of the nation. The most brutal damage occurred in New Orleans, Louisiana. Levee systems failed, flooding canal systems and entire neighborhoods. Engineer Karen Lahare was one of the many professionals who stepped in to help repair the systems. She managed a huge canal cleanup project in Louisiana. She and her team cleared more than 70 miles (113 km) of the canal system.

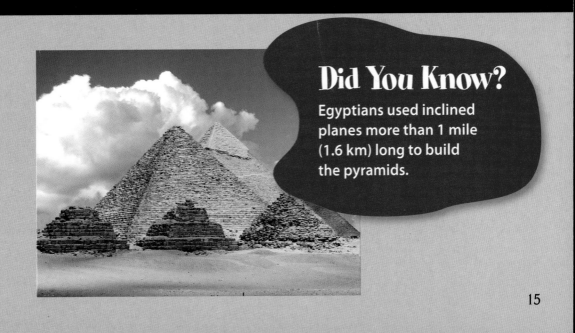

Did You Know?

Egyptians used inclined planes more than 1 mile (1.6 km) long to build the pyramids.

In 1797, 32-year-old Robert Fulton began looking for new opportunities. In Paris, France, he met American scholar Joel Barlow, who tutored him in mathematics and physics. Fulton also painted Barlow's portrait during that time.

Then Napoléon, the emperor of France, asked Fulton to design a practical submarine. Fulton's diving boat, as it was called, wasn't the first underwater vessel. A submarine had been used during the American Revolutionary War. But Fulton wanted to equip his with bombs so the submarine could sneak up on and destroy enemy warships. He hoped nations would stop attacking one another if such a fearsome vessel existed.

Fulton's design was called the *Nautilus*. To pay for his project, Fulton painted an enormous panorama inside a domed building. Tall canvasses were mounted on concealed rollers. Fulton's painting, called the *Burning of Moscow*, rolled by, making the story in art come to life. Panoramas were a popular form of entertainment at that time. Fulton made huge profits that paid for the *Nautilus*.

Modern Submarines

Submarines were first used extensively during World War I and World War II. In 1954, the first nuclear-powered submarine was developed. It could stay under water for long periods, allowing sailors to live below the sea for months at a time. Early submarines had to surface to fire missiles. Later submarines were able to fire underwater missiles that traveled long distances to their targets.

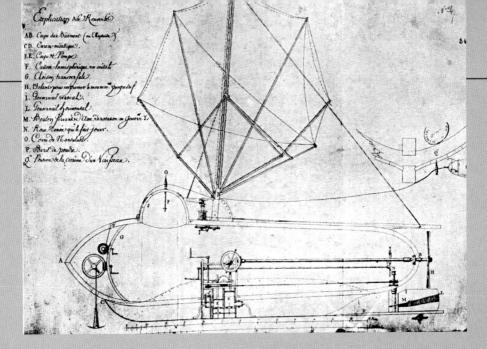

Fulton knew that submarines would be used for sea warfare, but he thought that they also might be used to stop piracy.

Modern submarines have been used for intelligence gathering, surveillance, and reconnaissance missions.

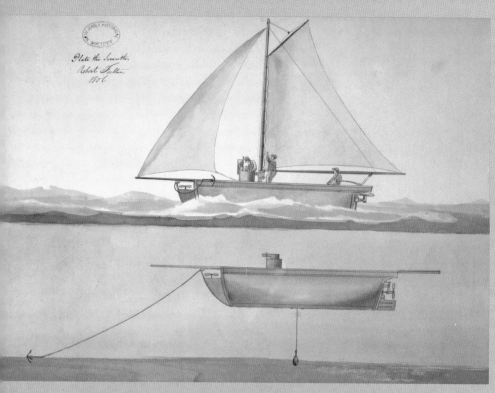

The French emperor Napoléon Bonaparte was impressed with Fulton's design of the *Nautilus* but never placed an order for the French army.

Fulton's submarine was impressive. The hull was armored to protect it from cannonballs. It was designed for a small crew of two or three men. They could stay underwater for long periods of time aided by Fulton's compressed air tanks that provided oxygen.

When the vessel was above water, the crew raised a mast and sail to power and guide it. The sail folded down when the craft submerged. Under water, the crew turned an inside crank to propel the sub through the water. The crew used a compass for direction.

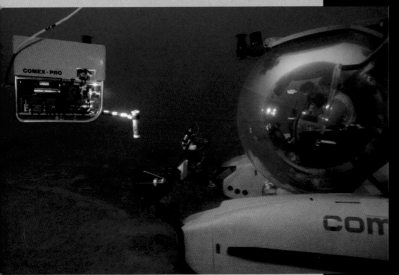

Robotic Submarin[es]

Today modern unmann[ed] underwater vehicles ca[n stay] submerged for much lo[nger] than the *Nautilus*. Thes[e] robotic vehicles patrol [the] seas, gathering data ab[out] sea life and informatio[n] about conditions deep [in] the ocean.

Naomi Leonard, engine[er] and professor of mecha[nical] and aerospace engineering, researches and designs miniat[ure] underwater robotic vehicles. Th[ese] tiny subs mimic the behavior o[f] schooling fish. Leonard recentl[y] received what is known as a "genius grant." She was awarde[d] $500,000 to fund her future wo[rk.] She was selected for her origina[l,] creativity, and potential to do [more.]

They observed what was going on above the water by looking through a periscope.

To test the *Nautilus*, Fulton and three people from the French government remained submerged in it for three hours. They lowered and raised the vessel by filling and emptying the water tanks. The sub could descend to depths of nearly 25 feet (7.6 meters). Water pressure at greater depths would have crushed the hull. Fulton also tested the vessel's wartime ability. He launched a torpedo, which destroyed a large sailboat.

The Steamboat

⬆ The Hudson River was originally called the North River. After the invention of the steamboat, the river became a popular place for leisure travel.

In 1802, Fulton met Robert Livingston, who introduced him to the steamboat. Livingston was the U.S. minister to France. He had landed a 20-year monopoly to provide steamboat service in the state of New York. But he had to develop a steamboat that could travel between New York and Albany at a speed of at least 4 miles (6.4 km) per hour. He had one year to complete the boat in order to keep the contract. He believed Robert Fulton was the person who could do it.

Livingston soon persuaded Fulton to give up his work on submarines and design a steamboat. Construction began on Fulton's steamboat in 1806. Charles Brownne was in charge of building the boat at a New York shipyard on the East River.

Monopoly

The steamboat monopoly was a huge moneymaker for Fulton and Livingston. It allowed them to seize any steamboat not licensed under the Fulton-Livingston company, and rivals were fined heavily for every trip made.

However, the monopoly delayed the wider introduction of the steamboat. In 1819, there were fewer than 10 steamboats on the Hudson River. In 1824, a Supreme Court decision overruled the monopoly and allowed other people to own and operate steamboats. By 1840, there were more than 100 steamboats in service.

Fulton tested his first steamboats on the Hudson River.

Improving an Old Idea

The steamboat was not a new idea in the early 1800s. Others had already tried to develop commercial steamboat travel. American William Henry had constructed a boat powered by steam in 1763.

In 1790, John Fitch built a steamboat that used a steam engine and several oars on each side to propel it. The boat carried passengers on the Delaware River between Philadelphia, Pennsylvania, and Trenton, New Jersey. But Fitch stopped the service when he decided that it wasn't making enough profit.

Fulton believed an inventor didn't have to have an entirely new idea to be successful. He built on past ideas and came up with better solutions.

While Fulton's steamboat was being built, angry boatmen tried to stop him. During the night, vandals would damage Fulton's boat, ramming the hull with their own boats. They were afraid steam-powered boats would put their sailboats, flatboats, and keelboats out of business. But Fulton had his boat repaired each time and hired men to guard it day and night.

The First Steam Engine

Thomas Savery (1650–1716) was a British inventor and military engineer. He built a steam engine that pumped water out of coal mines. He also designed an early paddle wheel that helped propel boats through the water.

Savery was the first person to use the word *horsepower* as a unit of measurement. He compared his engine's power to that of 10 horses.

Savery's pump used pressurized steam to force water upwards. However, the distance water could be pushed was limited by the pressure let off by the steam. Because of the high pressure required to run it, Savery's pump was not very safe.

Fulton designed his boat for maximum speed. He streamlined the shape and placed the paddle wheels in the best spots. Fulton asked engineers Boulton and Watts to modify their steam engine to make it more powerful. He gave them a diagram to show them what he wanted.

The steam engine worked by cycling hot and cold steam inside a main cylinder. The energy from the heat pushed a piston up and down. This powered the paddle wheels attached to the boat.

Fulton's steamboat made its maiden voyage on August 17, 1807. Then it began making regular trips on the Hudson River. Fulton officially registered his boat as the *North River Steamboat*. The boat was later rebuilt and renamed the *North River Steamboat of*

Measure Up

Fulton's design for the *North River Steamboat* took good mechanical engineering skills, including precise measurements.

Measurements of the *North River Steamboat*:

Length: 146 feet (45 m)

Width: 12 feet (4 m)

Cabin height: 6 ½ feet (2 m)

Average speed: 5 miles (8 km) per hour

Cost of the *North River Steamboat*:

Fulton and Livingston shared the following costs of the *North River Steamboat* in 1807:

Building the hull: $1,666

Steam engine: $2,750

Shipping and storage: $5,122

Clermont, after Livingston's Hudson River home. Although some people referred to the steamboat as the *Clermont*, Fulton preferred to call it the *North River*.

Fulton believed his steamboat could benefit the world. Although it was not the first steamboat, it proved to be the most economical, practical, and commercially successful. The steamboat ushered in a new era in commercial water transportation, carrying passengers and goods until 1814.

THE DEMOLOGOS OR FULTON THE FIRST.

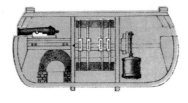

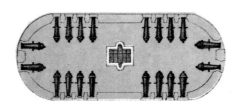

Fulton designed the *Demologos*, the first steam powered warship, in 1814. The ship was meant to be used during the War of 1812, but because the war ended before the ship's completion, it never saw any battles.

The first Steam Vessel of War in the World.

Fulton's Legacy

The *North River Steamboat of Clermont* was a huge success. Fulton and Livingston made $1,000 in profits in the first three months. Their steamboat business grew quickly. Their boats operated all along the East Coast and on the Mississippi River from New Orleans to Natchez, Mississippi. By 1815, Fulton and Livingston had 13 steamboats in commercial use. Fulton also constructed a steam-powered warship for the U.S. Navy.

But Fulton wouldn't live to see the huge impact his boats would have on the world. He died of pneumonia on February 23, 1815, at the age of 49. Fulton was survived by his wife, Harriet (who was Robert Livingston's niece), and four children.

Fulton would never know that steamboats flourished for more than a century after his death. In about 1920, railroads began offering faster travel and more destinations.

In the 1800s, steamboats did much of the work that modern ferries do today.

A statue of Robert Fulton holding a model of his steamboat sits in the U.S. Capitol. It was donated by the state of Pennsylvania.

Robert Fulton used his curiosity and intelligence to change travel and commerce forever. He was a new kind of inventor, improving on something that already existed. His first invention, the *North River Steamboat of Clermont*, would leave its mark on the world and pave the way for a golden age of commercial river travel.

Robotocist: Cynthia Breazeal

Massachusetts Institute of Technology

Robuddies

Have you ever seen a lifelike robot that could walk, talk, and make human expressions? Meet the woman who builds them. "I want robots to share our world with us, to communicate and interact with us, understand and even relate to us in a personal way," said Cynthia Breazeal.

Breazeal uses her know-ledge in mechanical and electrical engineering, psychology, computer programming, and even cartooning to build her robots. She said, "I want to be learning and creating all my life. That's why I went into engineering."

Speaking of learning, Breazeal's robots are learning, too. Her robot Kismet can communicate in a humanlike way, using microphones and sensors to hear and see. Breazeal builds other robots that can climb over rocky surfaces, figure out how to play with toys like Slinkies, and maybe someday think for themselves.

Breazeal's robot Leonardo is programmed to behave like a friend.

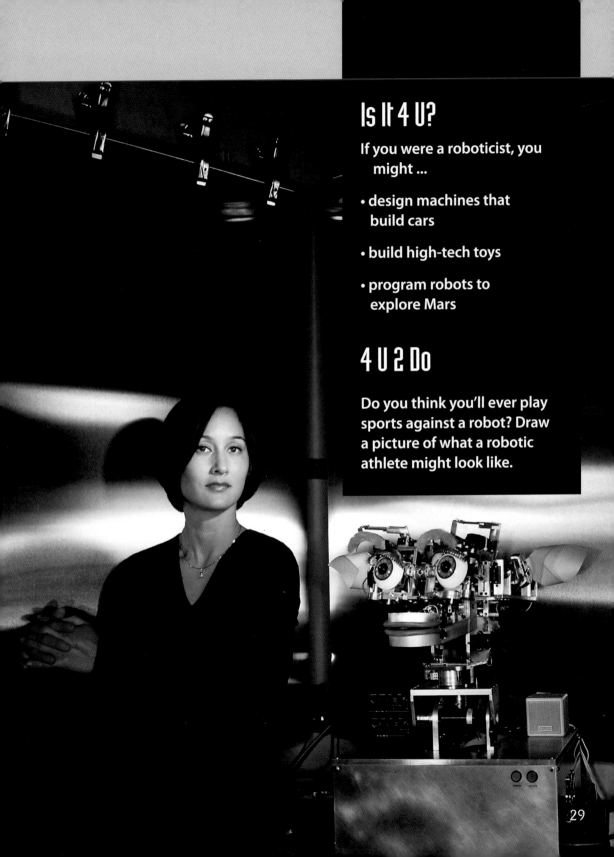

Is It 4 U?

If you were a roboticist, you might …

- design machines that build cars

- build high-tech toys

- program robots to explore Mars

4 U 2 Do

Do you think you'll ever play sports against a robot? Draw a picture of what a robotic athlete might look like.

30

Name:	Robert Fulton
Date of birth:	November 14, 1765
Nationality:	American
Birthplace:	Little Britain (now Fulton), Lancaster County, Pennsylvania
Parents:	Robert Fulton Sr., Mary Fulton
Spouse:	Harriet Livingston
Children:	Robert, Julia, Mary, Cornelia
Date of death:	February 24, 1815
Place of burial:	Trinity Churchyard, New York
Field of study:	Engineering
Known for:	First to design a steamboat that was a commercial success
Contributions to science:	Development of a submarine and commercial steamboat
Awards and honors:	A marble statue of Robert Fulton stands in the National Statuary Hall Collection in the U.S. Capitol
Publications:	*A Treatise on the Improvement of Canal Navigation*, 1796; *Report on the Practicability of Navigating With Steamboats on the Southern Waters of the United States*, 1813

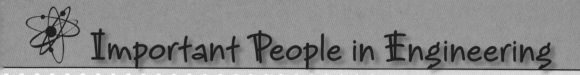

John Fitch (1743–1798)
Built a working steamboat before Robert Fulton but couldn't get funding to support it; a liberty ship (a mass-produced cargo ship) was named in his honor during World War II

Naomi Leonard (1963–   )
Marine roboticist who received a "genius grant" of $500,000 to continue her work designing ways to control underwater robot vehicles; her miniature underwater vehicles mimic the behavior of schooling fish

Cyrus McCormick (1809–1884)
Used his father's research to design and build a horse-drawn reaping machine that combined all the steps that other harvesting machines performed separately; it allowed farmers to increase their crop sizes with little or no additional effort

Lillian Moller Gilbreth (1878–1972)
Called the "First Lady of Engineering," Gilbreth experimented with time and motion, and advised several U.S. presidents on how to make work and defense more efficient; she was the first woman elected to the National Academy of Engineering; her family was the subject of the humorous books *Cheaper by the Dozen* and *Belles on Their Toes*

Sir Isaac Newton (1643–1727)
English mathematician and physicist who is called the most influential scientist who ever lived; described universal gravitation and the three laws of motion that came to be called Newton's laws; built the first practical refracting telescope

John Roebling (1806–1869)
Designed the Brooklyn Bridge, the world's longest suspension bridge at the time; he contracted tetanus after an accident, dying 24 days later; his son, Washington, took over the project; after Washington's death in 1872, Roebling's daughter-in-law, Emily, saw the project out until its end in 1883

Thomas Savery (1650–1715)
English inventor who designed the first steam engine in 1698 and published information about this pumping machine in his book *Miner's Friend*

James Watt (1736–1819)
Partner in the engineering firm Boulton and Watt who modified his steam engine for Robert Fulton's steamboat; Watt built his first steam engine without having seen a working model

Eli Whitney (1765–1825)
Invented the cotton gin, an automated machine designed to remove the seeds from cotton fibers; promoted the concept of mass production by promoting the use of interchangable parts in gun manufacturing

apprentice—person who works for and learns from a skilled tradesperson for a certain amount of time

canal—long channel of water artificially made for boats to travel along

compass—device for finding direction using a freely moving needle that always points to magnetic north

engineer—someone who plans, builds, or manages a building or construction project

flatboat—boat with a flat bottom and square ends, used for transporting freight in shallow water

graphite—soft, shiny black carbon used to make pencil lead

hull—body or frame of a ship, most of which goes under the water

inclined plane—simple machine for elevating objects

keelboat—large wooden riverboat with a cabin built in the center

laws of motion—Sir Isaac Newton's three basic laws that describe the effects of force on motion

monopoly—situation in which there is only one supplier of a good or service, and therefore that supplier can control the price

patent—grant made by a government giving an inventor the right to be the only one to make, use, or sell an invention for a certain number of years

shipyard—place where ships are built and repaired

steamboat—boat that moves by steam power

steam engine—engine that converts the heat energy of pressurized steam into mechanical energy

submarine—ship that can travel under water

warship—military ship designed for combat

1765	Robert Fulton is born in Little Britain, Lancaster County, Pennsylvania
1778	Constructs his first paddle wheel, which he attaches to fishing boats
1779	Moves to Philadelphia to apprentice with a jeweler
1782	Begins his miniature portrait business
1786	Travels to London, England, to study art with Benjamin West
1791	Two of Fulton's paintings are displayed at the Royal Academy of Arts in London
1793	Begins designing steam-powered ships
1796	Writes a book about canals called *Treatise on the Improvement of Canal Navigation*
1797	George Washington receives a copy of Fulton's book and writes Fulton a letter suggesting the possibility of canal navigation between Philadelphia and Lake Erie; Fulton meets scholar Joel Barlow, who teaches him about mathematics and physics; Fulton paints Barlow's portrait; paints the *Burning of Moscow*, the first panoramic painting ever shown in Paris; designs the *Nautilus*, a submarine designed to destroy enemy warships

1798	Begins a project to improve canals and canal navigation
1799	Receives a patent from the British government for his double-inclined plane, which can raise or lower boats from one canal level to another
1800	Pilots the *Nautilus* for nearly 20 minutes in 25 feet (7.6 m) of water
1801	Tests his first submarine in France and destroys a sailboat with a torpedo
1802	Robert Livingston obtains a monopoly on all steamboats operating on the Hudson River
1803	Launches a steamboat; it immediately sinks; the engine and boiler are salvaged and used in another boat, but Fulton is disappointed with the results
1805	While conducting experiments with an improved submarine, the underwater ship sinks
1807	Designs a commercial steamboat, the *North River Steamboat*, to transport passengers between Albany, New York, and New York City
1808	Livingston convinces the New York Legislature to renew his Hudson River monopoly contract, adding an additional five years for every new boat launched

1809	Obtains a patent for his steamboat, registering it as the *North River Steamboat of Clermont*
1811	Builds a new type of steamboat with a paddle wheel near the rear of the boat; he calls it the *New Orleans*
1812	Builds the first steam-powered warship called the *Demologos*
1815	Fulton and Livingston own 13 steamboats for commercial use in their steamboat business; Fulton contracts pneumonia and dies
1824	Fulton and Livingston's monopoly on the Hudson River steamboats is found unconstitutional by the U.S. Supreme Court

Additional Resources

Flamming, James M. *Robert Fulton: Inventor and Steamboat Builder*. Berkeley Heights, N.J.: Enslow Publishers Inc., 1999.

Parks, Peggy J. *Robert Fulton: Innovator With Steam Power*. San Diego: Blackbirch Press, 2004.

Rebman, Renée C. *Robert Fulton's Steamboat*. Minneapolis: Compass Point Books, 2008.

Sale, Kirkpatrick. *The Fire of His Genius: Robert Fulton and the American Dream*. New York: Free Press, 2001.

Whiting, Jim. *Robert Fulton*. Hockessin, Del.: Mitchell Lane Publishers, 2007.

Zimmerman, Karl. *Steamboats: The Story of Lakers, Ferries, and Majestic Paddlewheelers*. Honesdale, Pa.: Boyds Mills Press, 2006.

On the Web

For more information on this topic, use FactHound.

1. Go to *www.facthound.com*

2. Type in this book ID: 0756539617

3. Click on the *Fetch It* button.

FactHound will find the best Web sites for you.

Index

Don Herweck

Don Herweck was born and educated in Southern California and has degrees in math, physics, and physical science. Currently he is an operations manager for a large automotive manufacturer and travels internationally and throughout the United States for his business. He is the father of four children and has recently returned to California after several years living in the South and Midwest.

Image Credits